STEPPARENTS

BY HOLLY DUHIG

KidHaven PUBLISHING

I0869272

Published in 2019 by KidHaven Publishing, an Imprint of Greenhaven Publishing, LLC
353 3rd Avenue, Suite 255, New York, NY 10010

© 2019 Booklife Publishing

This edition is published by arrangement with Booklife Publishing.

All rights reserved. No part of this book may be reproduced in any form
without permission in writing from the publisher, except by a reviewer.

Written by: Holly Duhig
Edited by: Kirsty Holmes
Designed by: Danielle Rippengill

Cataloging-in-Publication Data

Names: Duhig, Holly.
Title: Stepparents / Holly Duhig.
Description: New York : KidHaven Publishing, 2019. | Series: Topics to talk about | Includes glossary and index.
Identifiers: ISBN 9781534526600 (pbk.) | ISBN 9781534526594 (library bound) | ISBN 9781534526617 (6 pack)
Subjects: LCSH: Stepparents--Juvenile literature. | Stepfamilies--Juvenile literature.
Classification: LCC HQ759.92 D84 2019 | DDC 306.874'7--dc23

Image Credits: All images are courtesy of Shutterstock.com, unless otherwise specified. With thanks to Getty Images, Thinkstock Photo and iStockphoto. Front Cover – szefei, prapann, Alexander Lysenko, Mc Satori, Kim Reinick, Yellow Cat, nafterphoto, Quang Ho, Madlen. Images used on every spread – Red_Spruce, MG Drachal, Alexander Lysenko, Kues, Flas100, Kanate, Mc Satori, Nikolaeva. 1 – szefei, prapann. 2 – Africa Studio. 4–7 – Africa Studio. 7 – alexmisu. 8 – Africa Studio. 9 – Photographee.eu, Filip Fuxa. 10 – Nopparat Nambunyen. 11 – Monkey Business Images, wavebreakmedia. 12 & 13 – Africa Studio. 14 – Tom Wang. 15 – Africa Studio. 16 – Joshua Resnick, udra11. 17 – Africa Studio. 18 – Brocreative. 19 – Africa Studio. 20 – Natalya Chumak. 21–23 – Africa Studio.

Printed in the United States of America

CPSIA compliance information: Batch #BS18KL: For further information contact Greenhaven Publishing LLC, New York, New York at 1-844-317-7404.

Contents

Words that look like **this** can be found in the glossary on page 24.

My Family

This is my family. There is me, my mom, my stepdad, and my stepbrother.

My name is Ella. My mom's name is Candice. For a long time, it was just me and her.

JOINING FAMILIES

When I was six, my mom introduced me to Alex and his son, Kurtis. She said she met Alex at her job and they really liked each other.

OUR HOUSE

ALEX AND KURTIS CAME TO OUR HOUSE TO PLAY.

After a while, Mom told me that Alex and Kurtis were going to come over to our house. I was really worried at first. I didn't want to have to share my mom with other people.

At first, Alex and Kurtis only came to our house on the weekends. It wasn't long before I started to look forward to seeing them again!

When they moved in, our spare room became Kurtis's room. It was very plain, so I helped him decorate it. He brought all his toys and games with him.

WEDDINGS

Last year, Mom and Alex decided to get married. I was a bridesmaid and Kurtis was a **ring bearer**.

I GOT TO HOLD FLOWERS.

My Step-Grandma and step-grandpa.

The wedding cake was delicious!

Lots of people came to the wedding. I got to meet the rest of Alex and Kurtis's family, including Kurtis's grandparents, who are now my step-grandparents.

Changing Names

When people get married, they often change their **surnames**. My mom changed her surname to match Alex's. They are now Mr. and Mrs. Hughes.

I changed my surname to Hughes, too. It made me feel like a part of our new family. Now my last name and Kurtis's last name match!

Lu Cháng is my best friend at school. She also has a stepdad, but she hasn't changed her name. This is because she mostly lives with her **birth parent** and wanted to keep the same surname as him.

It's always just been me and Mom, so I used to have her surname. When she changed her name, I wanted to change mine, too.

FAMILY LIFE

It was difficult getting used to having a stepfamily at first. I didn't like it when Alex told me to clean my room, and Kurtis didn't like it when my mom made him do his homework.

I now know that Alex just wants to look after me like a father. Sometimes he asks me to do chores, but other times he takes me to fun things like dance class.

Family Fun

We go lots of fun places as a family. One time we visited the **aquarium**. We saw sharks!

Even though Alex and Kurtis live with us, Mom still takes me to cool places when it's just the two of us.

NEW BEGINNINGS

The best thing about our family is that it's still growing. My mom and Alex have decided to have a baby together.

The new baby will be mine and Kurtis' **half-sibling**.
There's been lots to do to get ready for a new baby.
I helped Mom and Alex paint the **nursery**.

Families are always growing and changing. This can be scary at first, but it can also be really exciting!

I love my mom, my stepdad, and my stepbrother – and I know I will love the new baby, too. I wouldn't change my family for the whole world!

Glossary and Index

Glossary

aquarium a place containing tanks of many different sea creatures

birth parent biological parent

half-sibling a sibling who shares one biological parent

nursery a room in a house for a baby or young child

ring bearer someone who carries the rings in a wedding

surname a last name that is passed down through the family

Index